I'm All Ready To Go

Little Timmy's first day of school

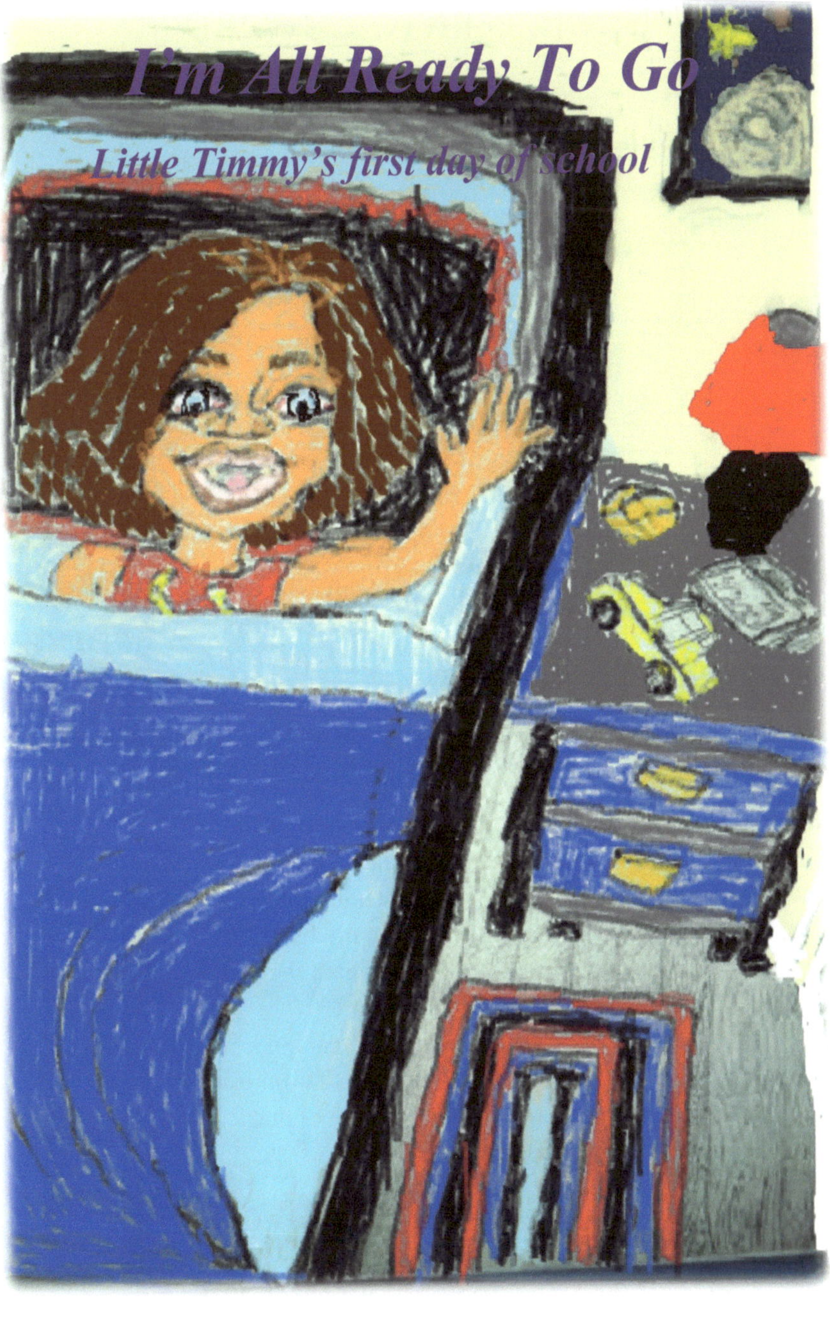

SHONLEEKA R. COWARD

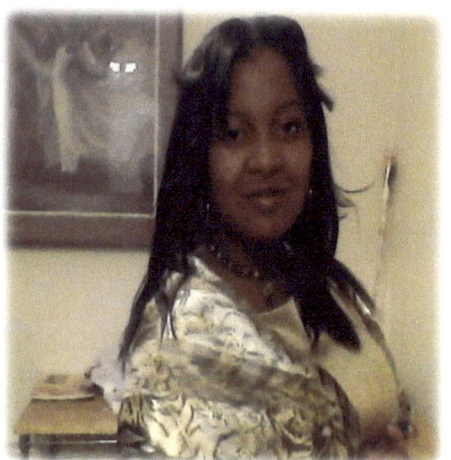

I'm All Ready to Go

Little Timmy First Day of School

2014

I came up with this story one night. When I was on my way to sleep. I can't sleep for a few hours. Because I was going over every detail in my head. From how I wanted to look. To how I wanted the story to end and begin. This story is about an African American boy that was only five years old. That could not wait to go to school for the first time. He was so excited about his first day of school that he woke up two hours early to start his day off.

Written,

Illustrated

&

Self-Published

By:

SHONLEEKA R.COWARD

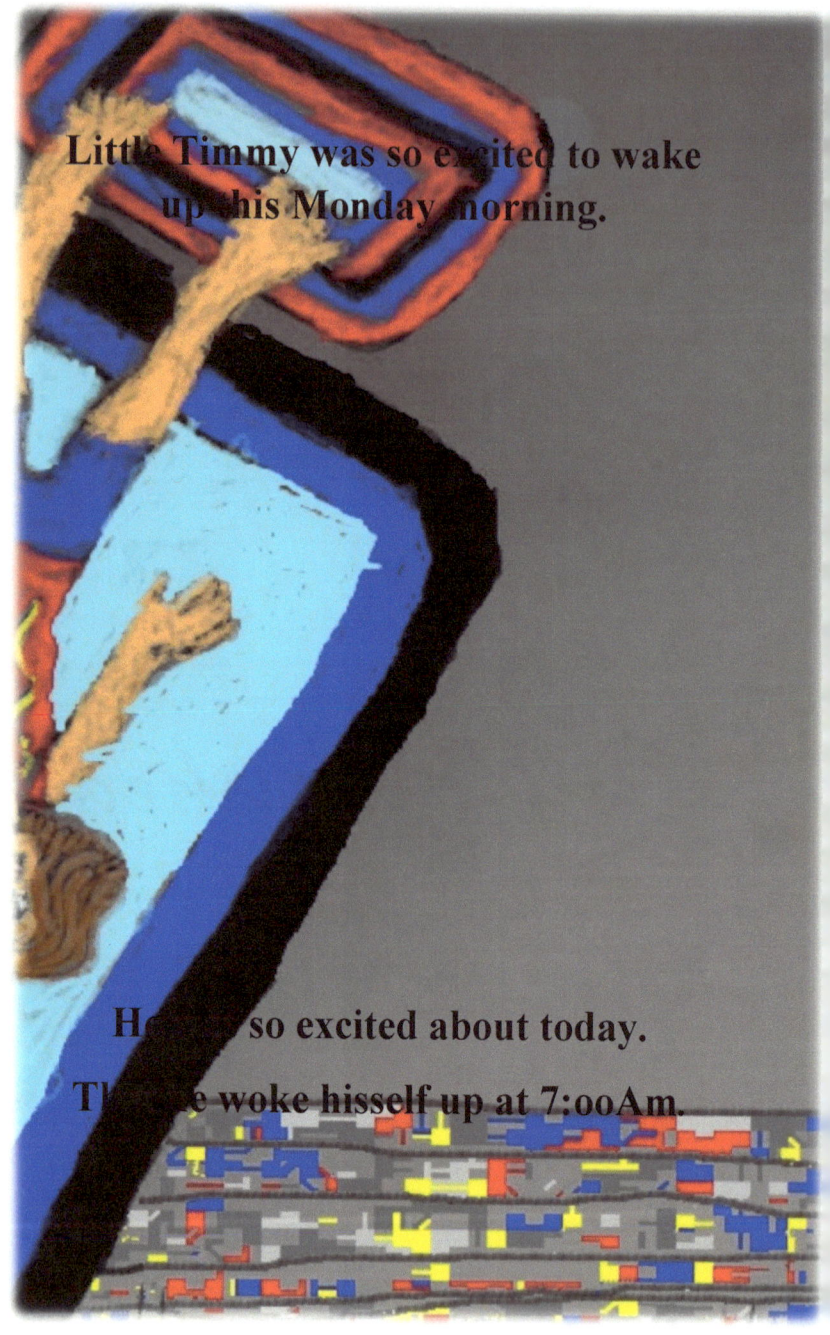

Little Timmy was so excited to wake up this Monday morning.

He was so excited about today.

That he woke hisself up at 7:ooAm.

Timmy's mom Tiffany heard Little Timmy moving around up stairs. And she started walking up the stairs to see what little Timmy was doing. Timmy are you ok? She yelled as she made it up the last stair. Yes, mommy.

Timmy Answered. Timmy what are you doing up so early? He answered

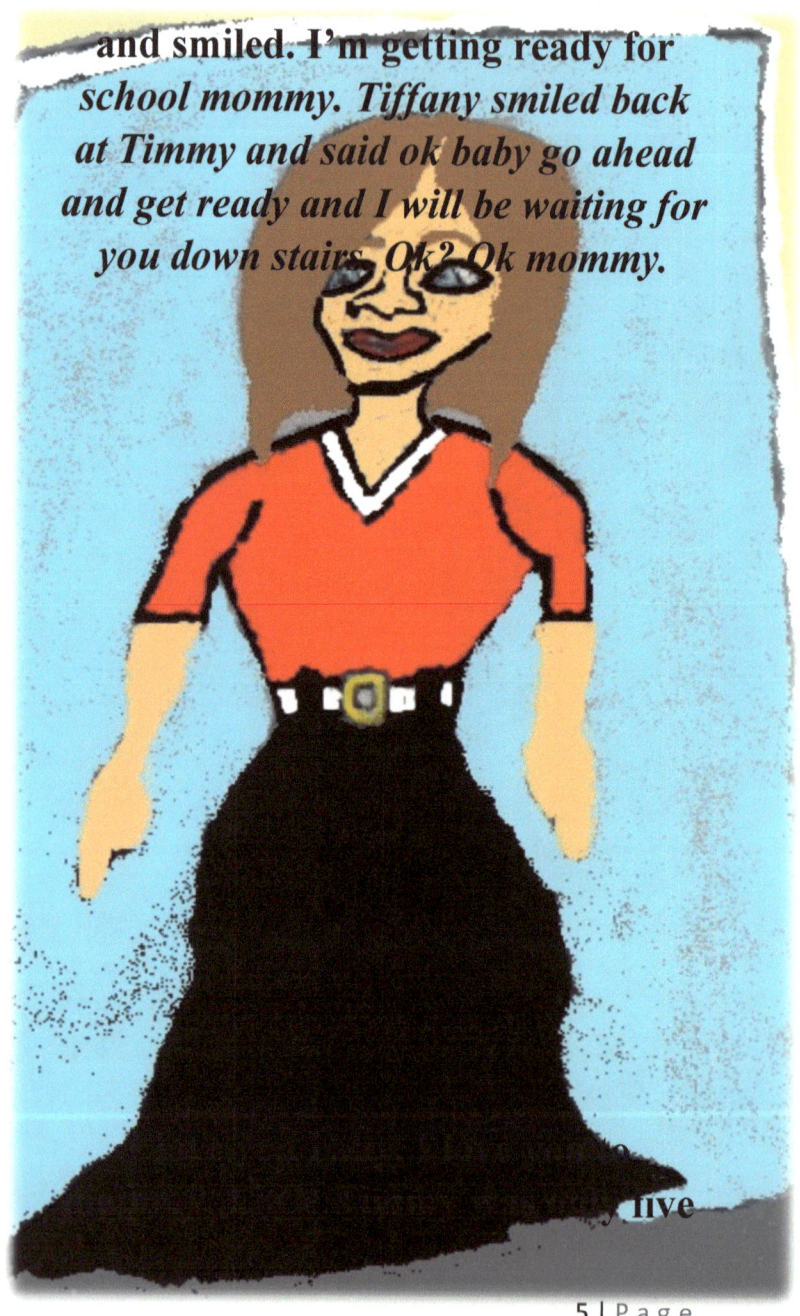

and smiled. I'm getting ready for school mommy. Tiffany smiled back at Timmy and said ok baby go ahead and get ready and I will be waiting for you down stairs. Ok? Ok mommy.

live

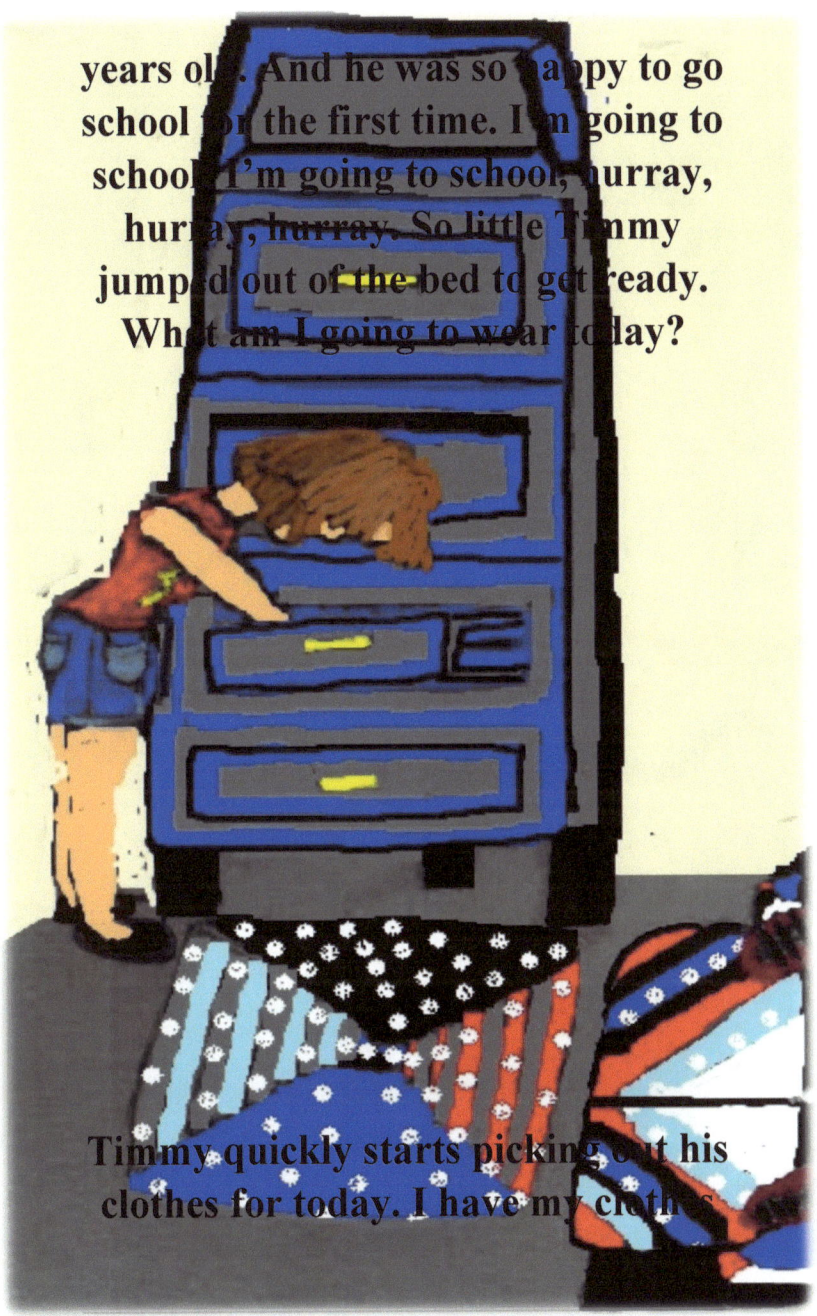

years old. And he was so happy to go school for the first time. I'm going to school I'm going to school, hurray, hurray, hurray. So little Timmy jumped out of the bed to get ready. What am I going to wear today?

Timmy quickly starts picking out his clothes for today. I have my clothes.

out mommy. Ok baby mommy made you some bath water.

Make sure you get in the tub ok. Do it have Mr. Bubbles in it mommy? Yes baby it does. Yay, bubbly, bubbly, bubbly.

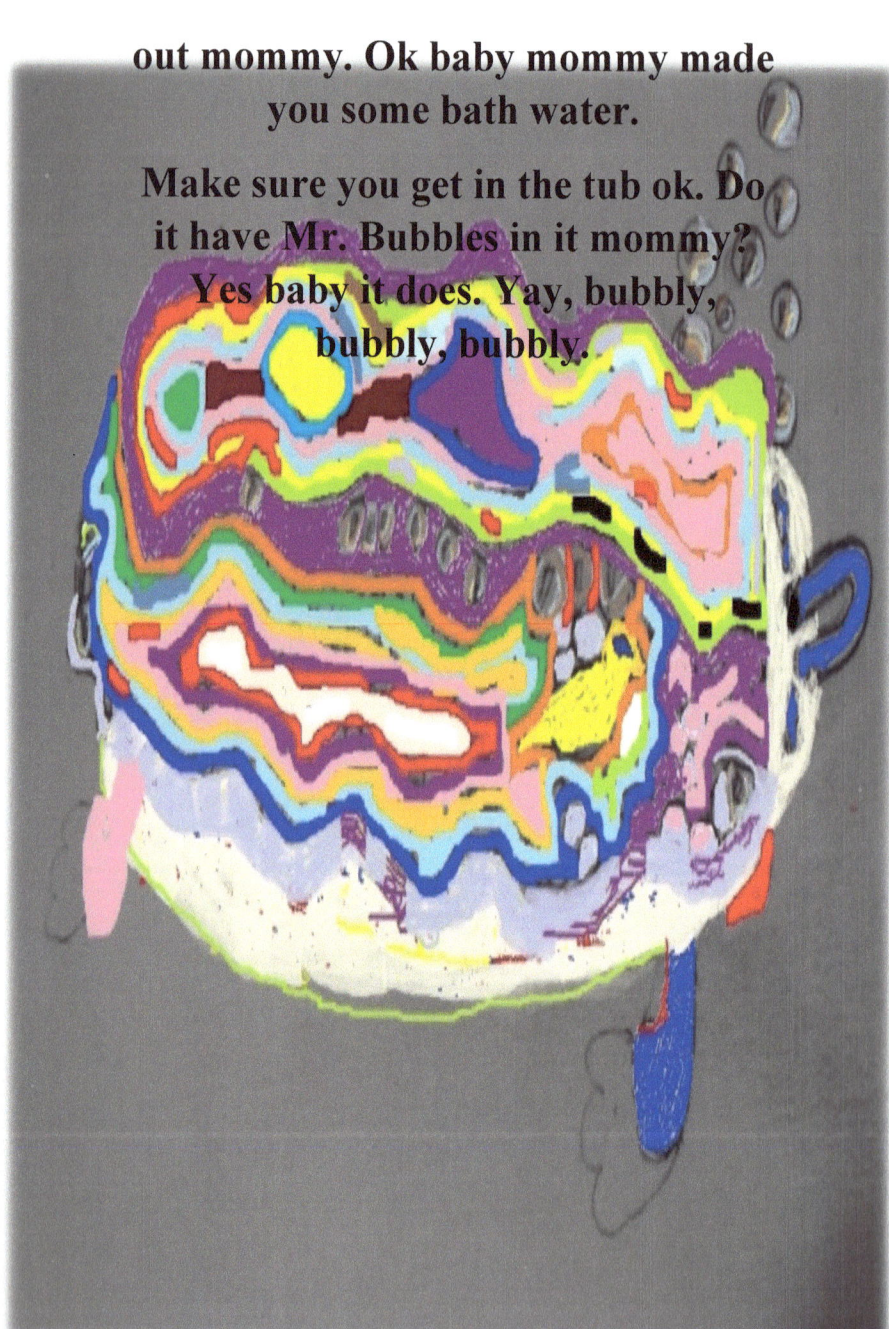

Then Little Timmy went in to the bath room to jump in the tub.

Tiffany Timmy's mom walks back up the stairs to see if Timmy needed some help in the tub. Honey do you need some help?

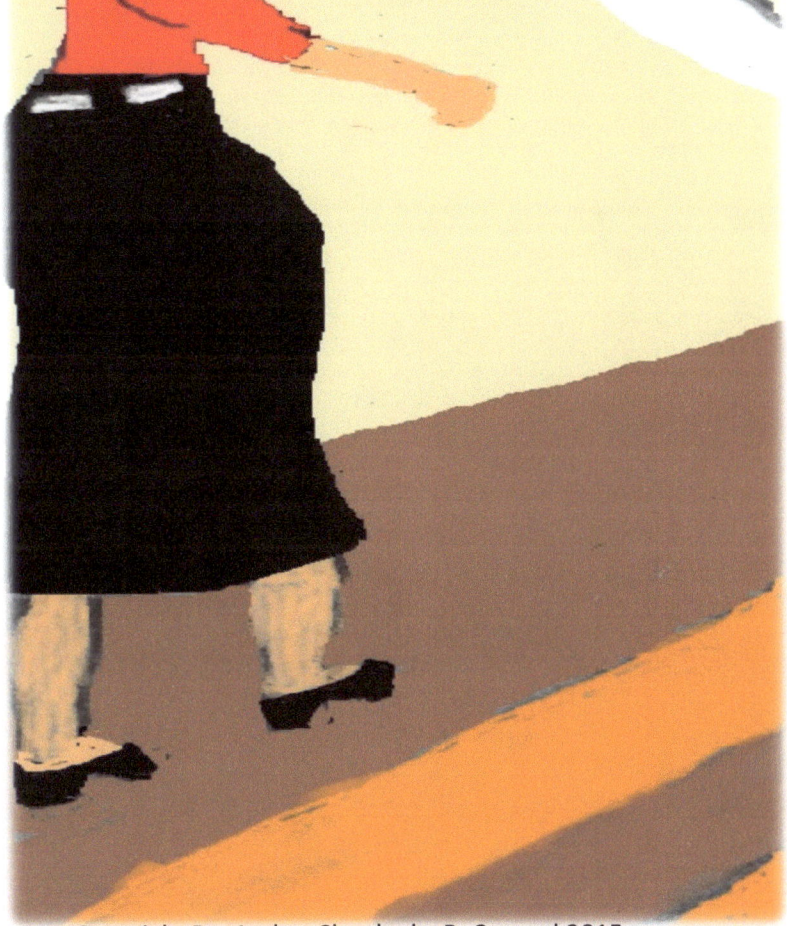

No, mommy I'm ok. Mommy, Yes baby?

Am I a big kid now? Yes, baby you are. Yay, I'm a big kid now. Ok baby and hurry up and get washed up so you want be late for the school bus.

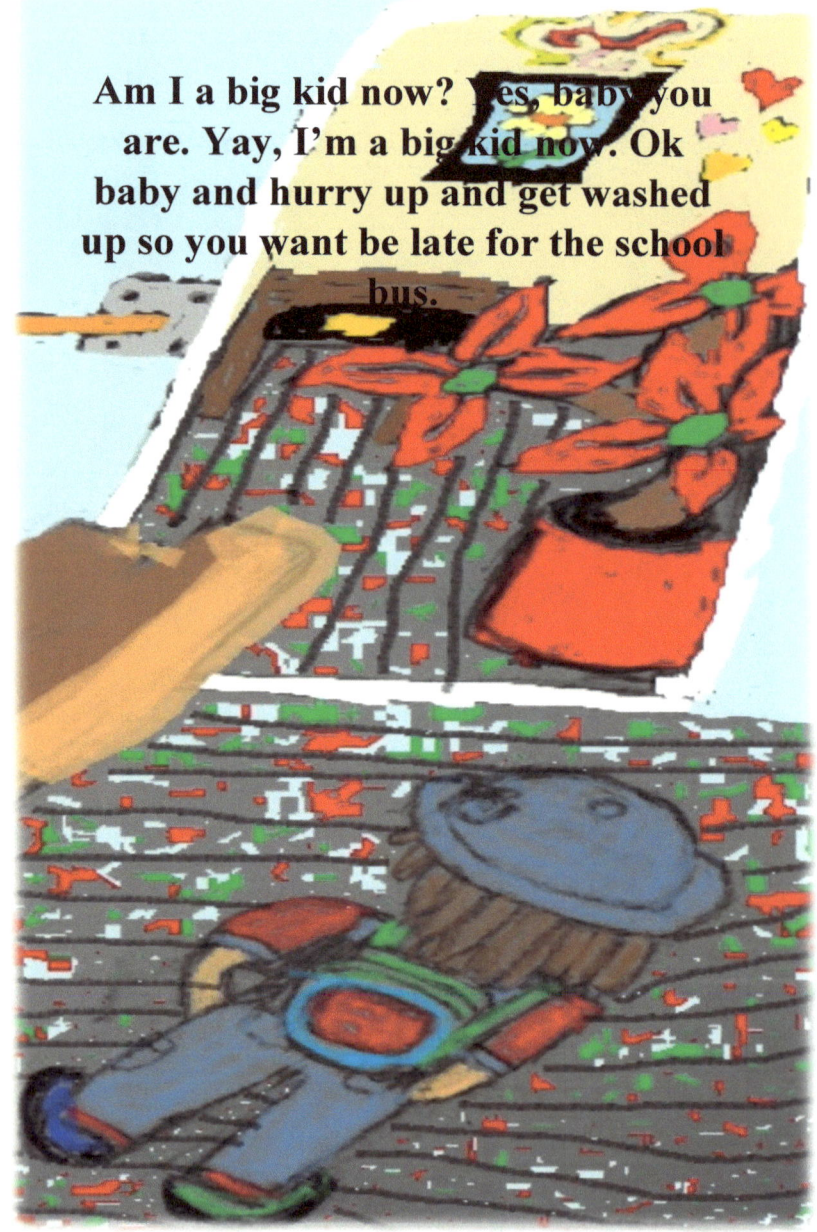

Ok mommy. Ok baby My baby is going to school. I am so happy. Timmy jumps out of the tub. And he *puts on his clothes on and walks down the stairs to eat breakfast. Ok I'm all ready to go mommy.*

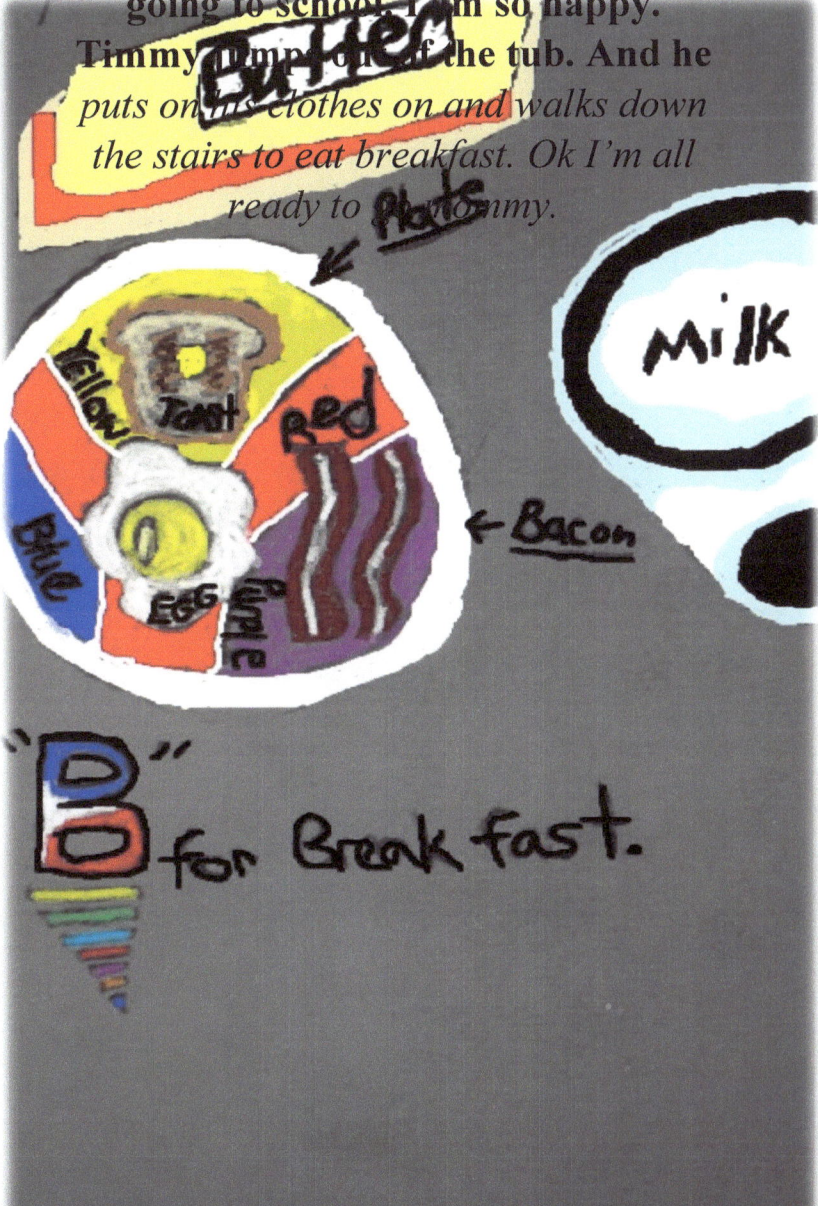

"B" for Breakfast.

Tiffany looks back at Timmy. Baby what you have on? My first day outfit. Tiffany start laughing and shaking her head. Baby you are just like me.

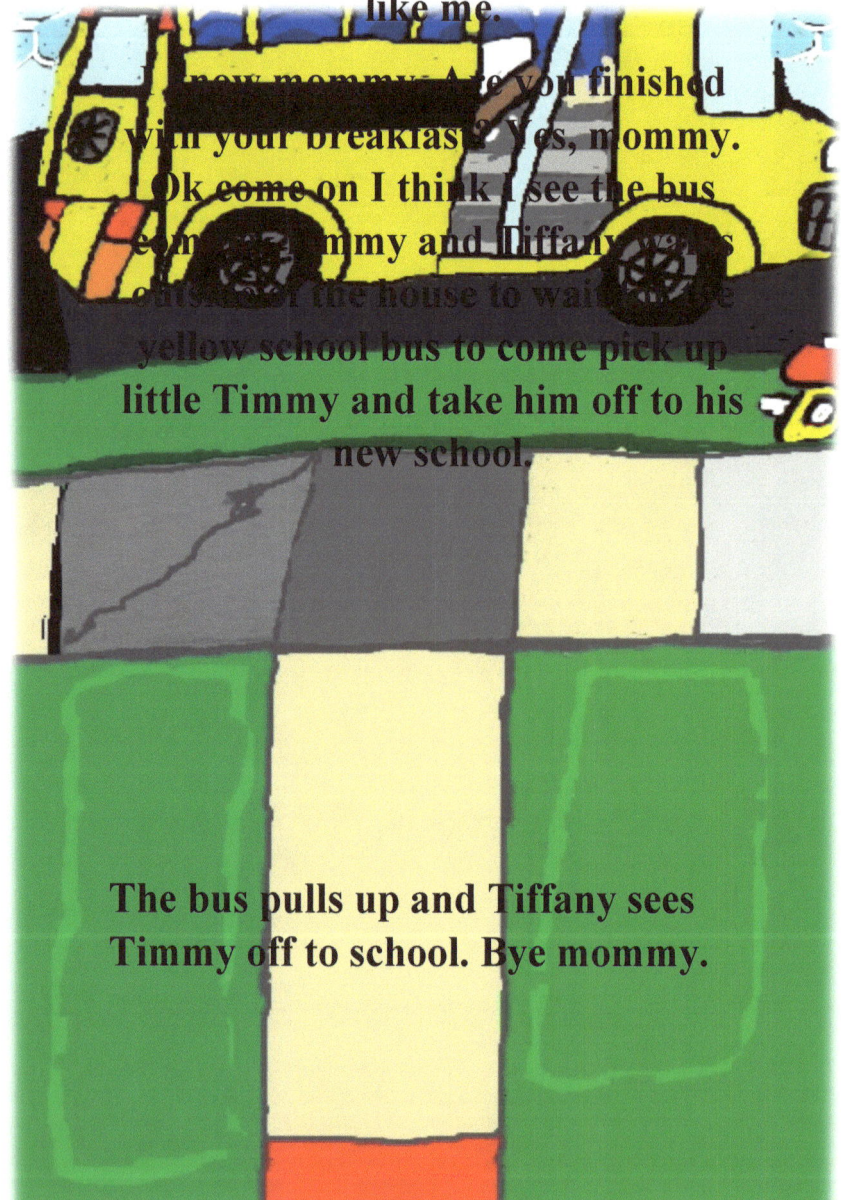

now mommy. Are you finished with your breakfast? Yes, mommy. Ok come on I think I see the bus com mmy and Tiffany walks outside of the house to wait for the yellow school bus to come pick up little Timmy and take him off to his new school.

The bus pulls up and Tiffany sees Timmy off to school. Bye mommy.

Bye baby and I will see you when you get home. Ok mommy. Love you baby and have fun. The bus pulls off and *Timmy is on his way to school for the first time.*

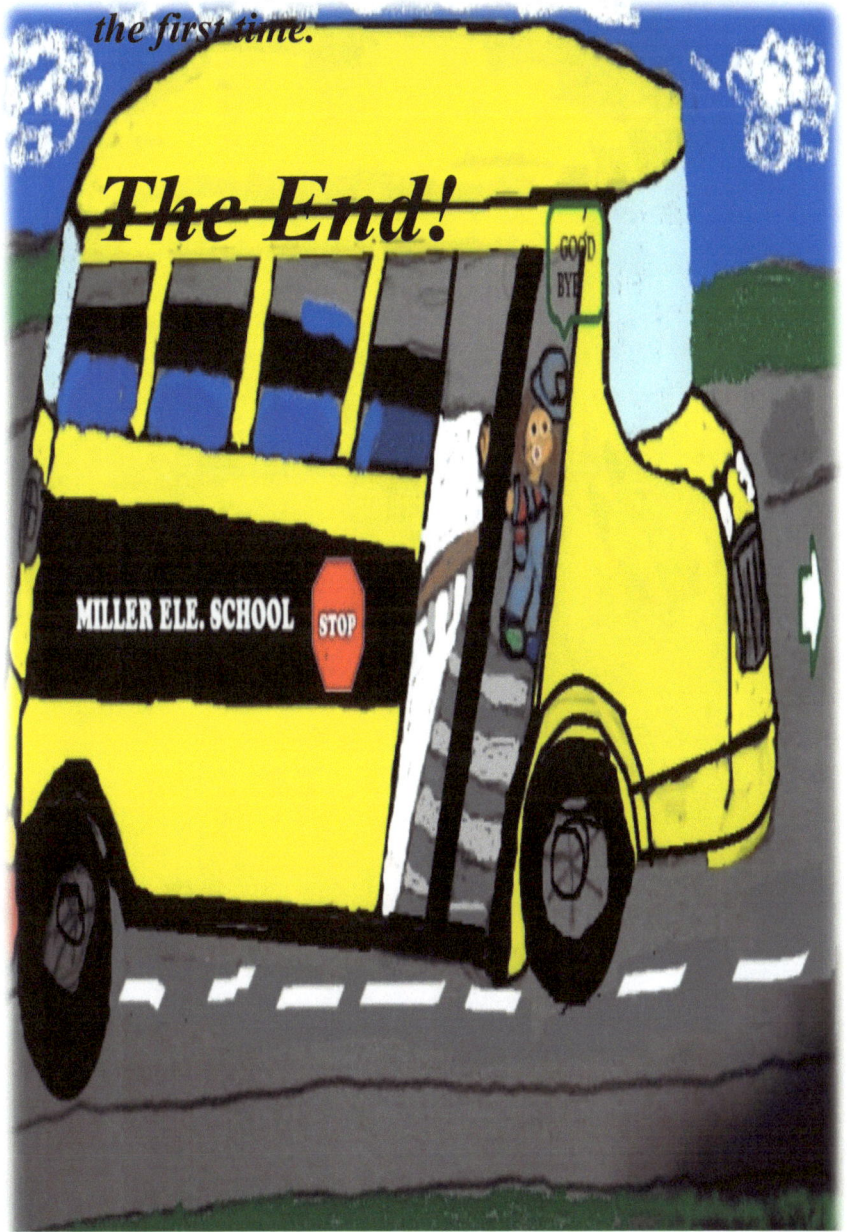

The End!

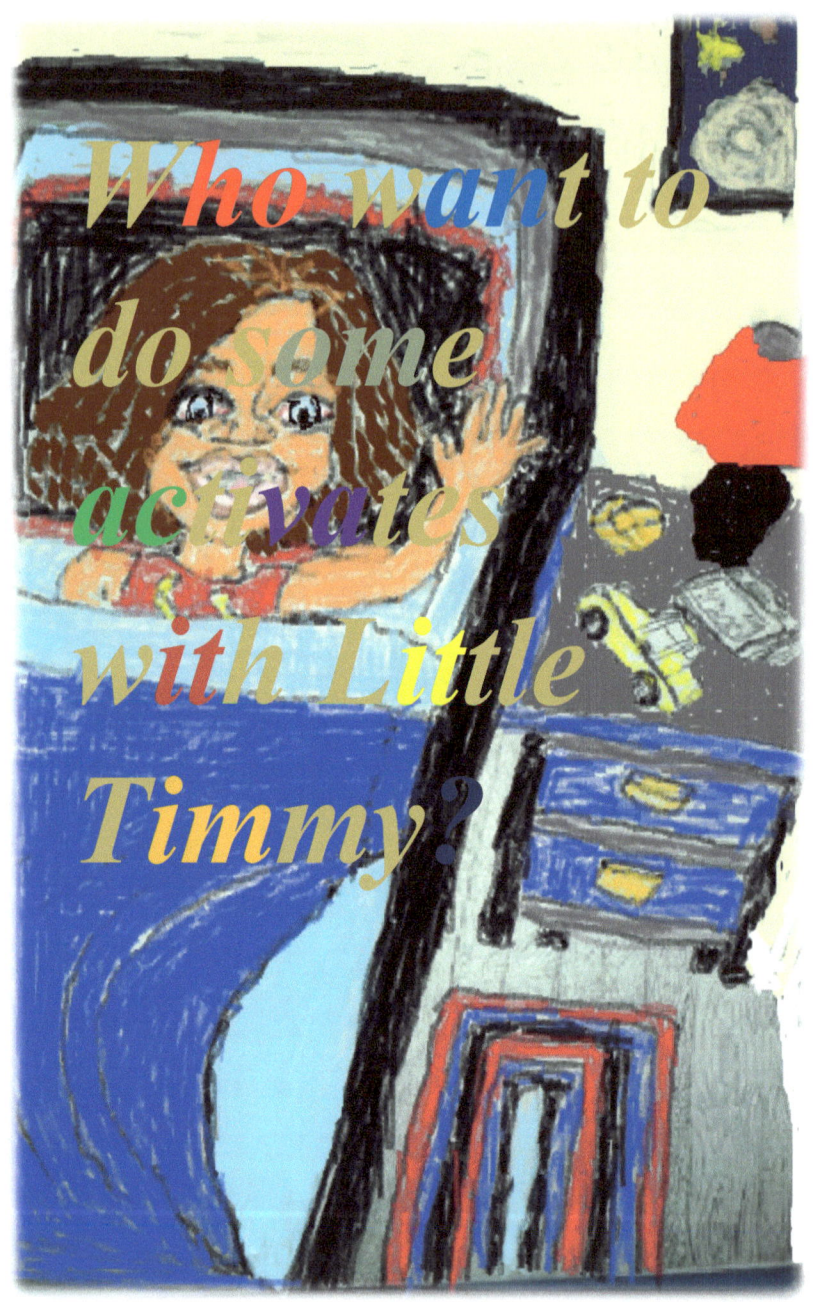

Little Timmy need some help with his Alphabets. Can you help Little Timmy song his Alphabets?

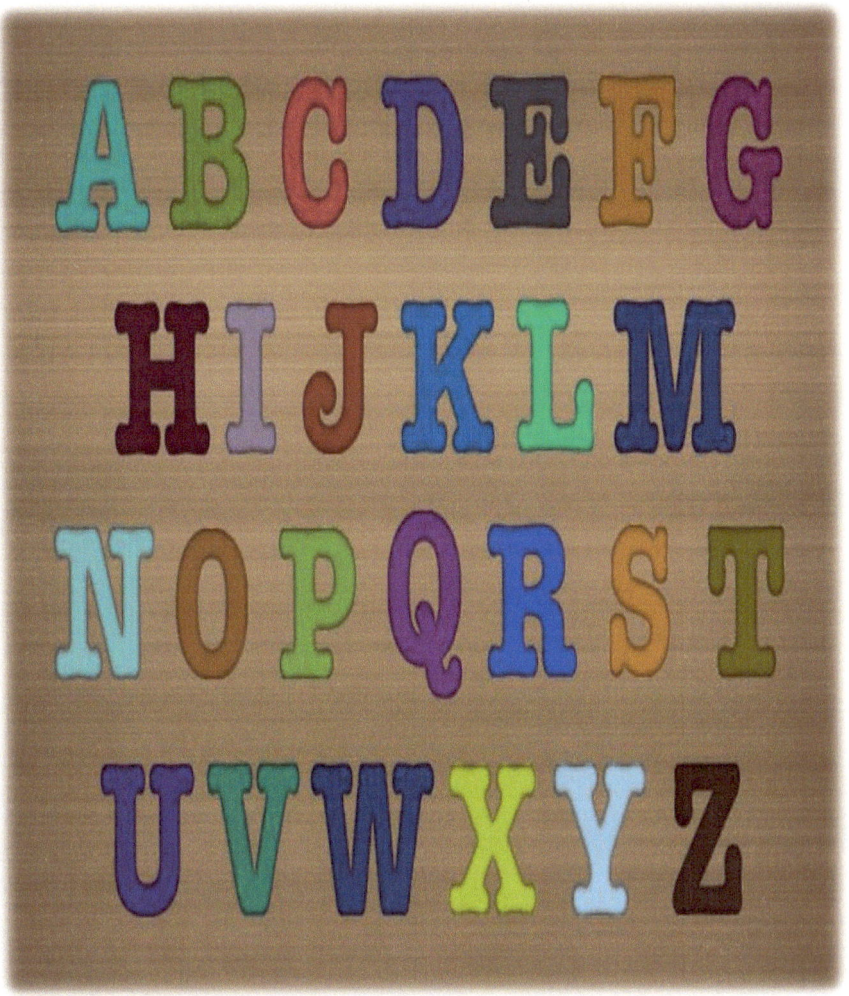

Little Timmy Bus driver is trying to find his way to Miller Elementary School. Can you help his find his way?

Add and Subtract the number's to find the anwser's to Problem's. Then color it according the answer code on the sied of your page.

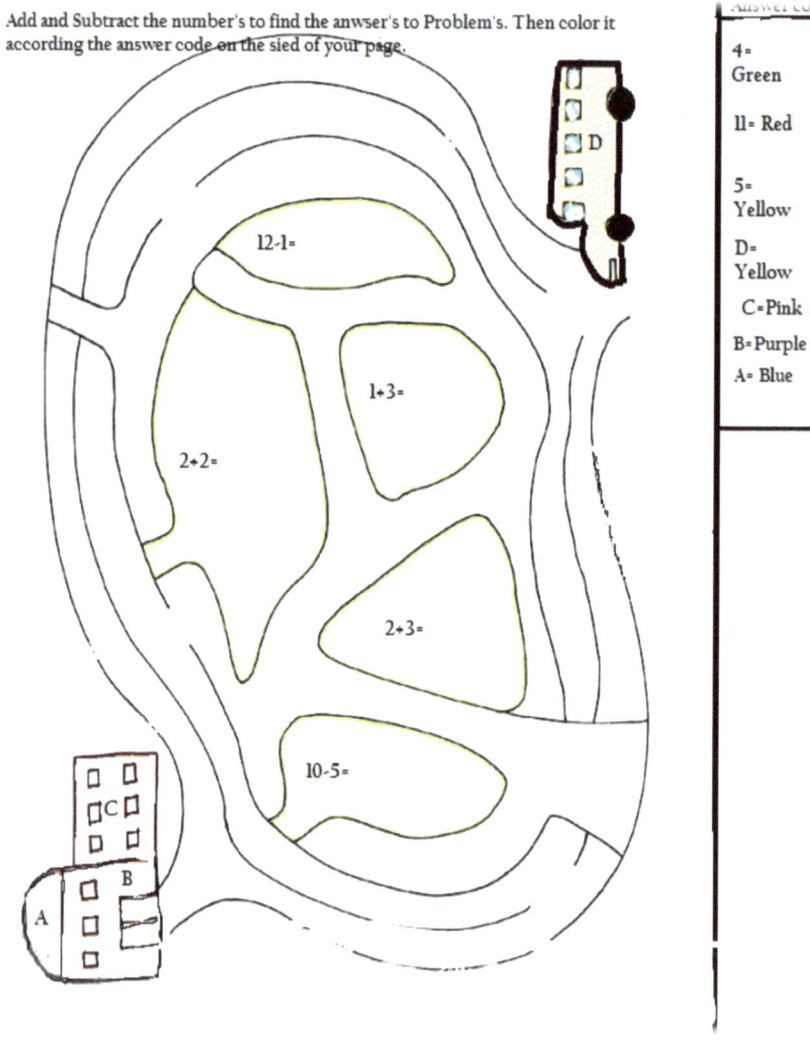

Answer code

4 = Green

11 = Red

5 = Yellow

D = Yellow

C = Pink

B = Purple

A = Blue

Little Timmy loves Dinosaur. So connect the Dots to help Little Timmy find his Dinosaur.

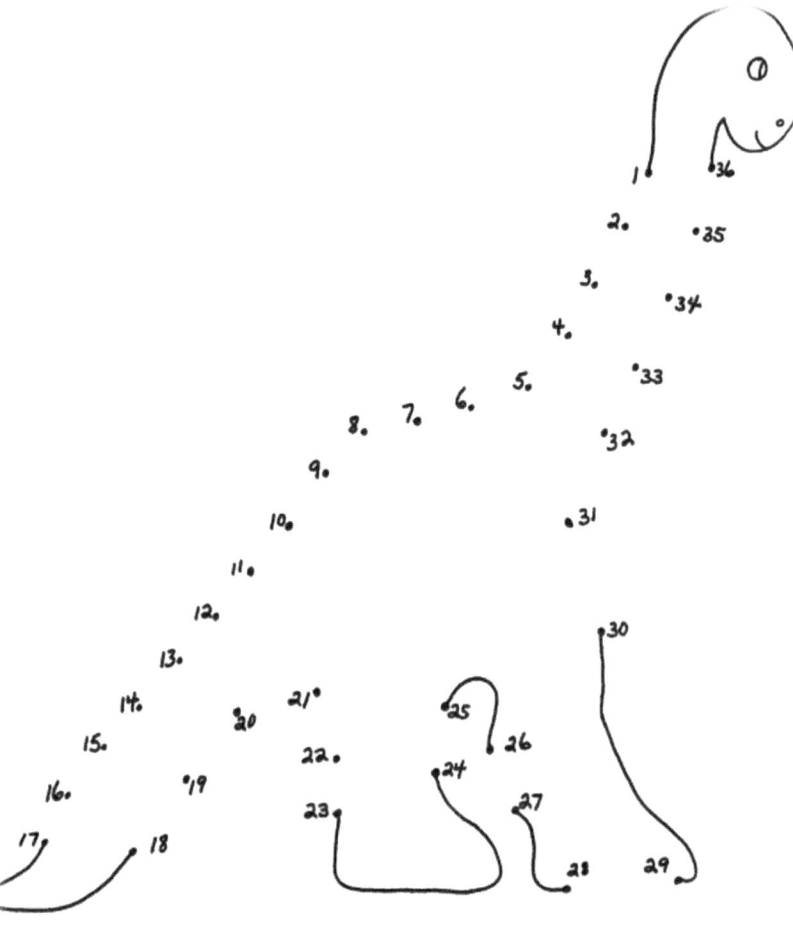

Brontosaurus

Little Timmy will love for you to learn the Sign Language Alphabet with him. So get ready.

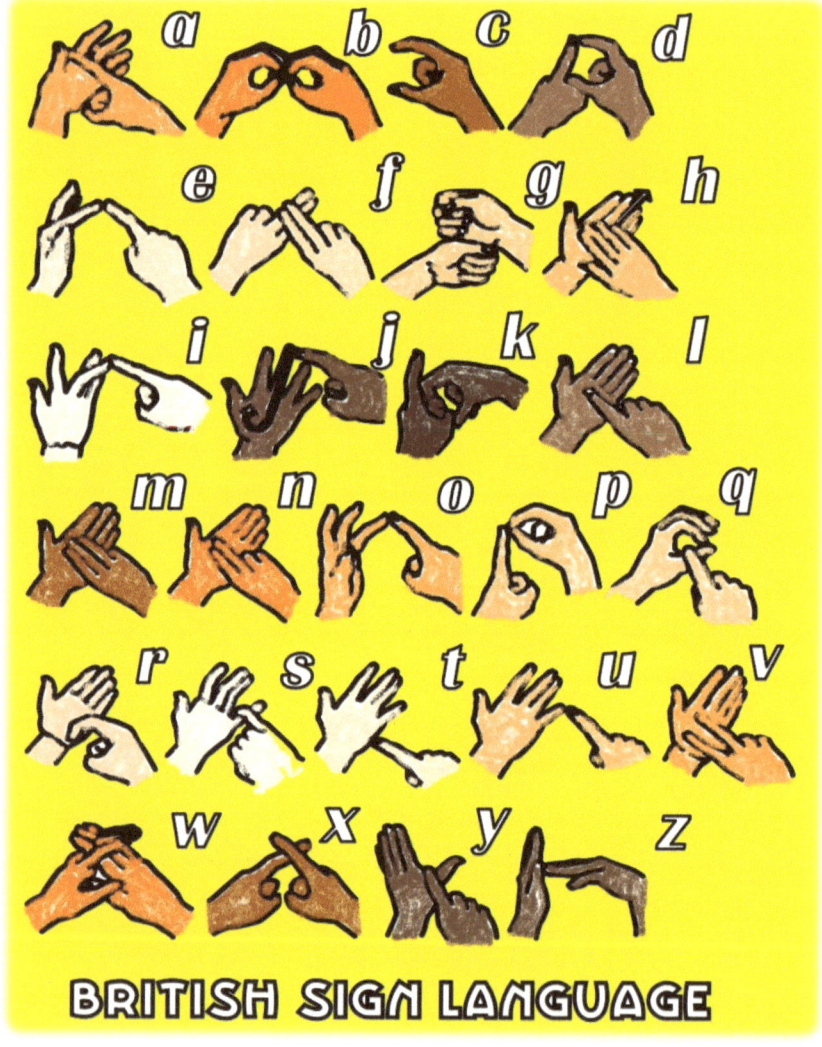

Little Timmy have some homework to do. And he wanted to know if you will like to help. He needs your help with tracing the numbers. Can you help him?

Tracing Numbers 1 - 10

1 2 3 4 5 6 7 8 9 10

1 2 3 4 5 6 7 8 9 10

1 2 3 4 5 6 7 8 9 10

1 2 3 4 5 6 7 8 9 10

Little Timmy needs help with fingering out his class work. Can you help him with his class work please?

Addition with sums up to 20
Sum and write the correct number in the box.

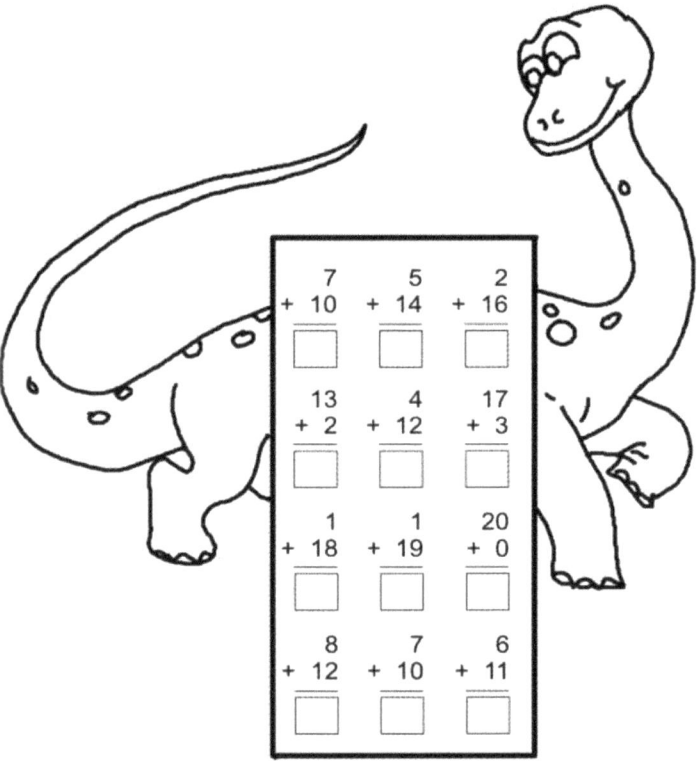

7 + 10	5 + 14	2 + 16
13 + 2	4 + 12	17 + 3
1 + 18	1 + 19	20 + 0
8 + 12	7 + 10	6 + 11

Hi I'm Little Timmy and I will love for you to learn shapes and colors with me.

Color all the rectangle shapes orange.

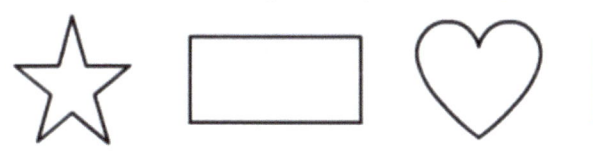

Color all the oval shapes green.

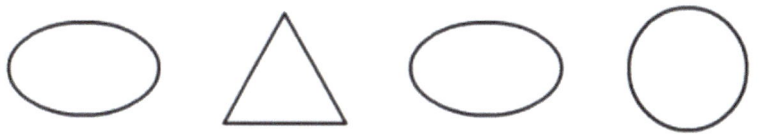

Color all the heart shapes red.

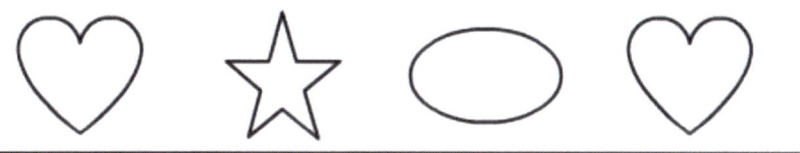

Color all the circle shapes pink.

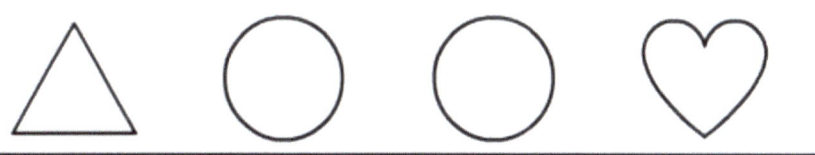

Color all the triangle shapes blue.

 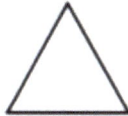 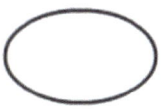 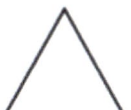

Little Timmy Words Of The Day

Family Words	
mom	
dad	
brother	
sister	

Little Timmy's Word Puzzle

Summer Search

```
D R P S U N T A N I C E C R E A M
Z F C H U S U N B U R N F N J E N
Y I A H G H B O A T C O U S U G B
W R U E F F I S H I N G O I N L E
M K G U T I B I K I N I C W E O A
N Q U B E E W A T E R M E L O N C
A N S W I M M I N G J L W G B B H
Y Q T A C I P Q T O U Q N J D O H
V R N N G X S G T W L X X G R L Y
A L T F C M F Q D P Y S D A P C D
C O L O A O A X G C M A I T P C E
A T W S M S N S U N G L A S S E S
T I O H P Q F X D F T E N T P X L
I O V O I U I W Q K R H O T B M C
O N J R N I M U F F H L K G L R W
N Z R T G T X J Z K L H A T X Z T
B K N S V O Q W J V X X R D W E B
```

August	hat	shorts
beach	hot	sunburn
bikini	ice cream	sunglasses
boat	July	suntan
camping	June	swimming
fan	lotion	tent
fishing	mosquito	vacation

www.boyslegoworld.com

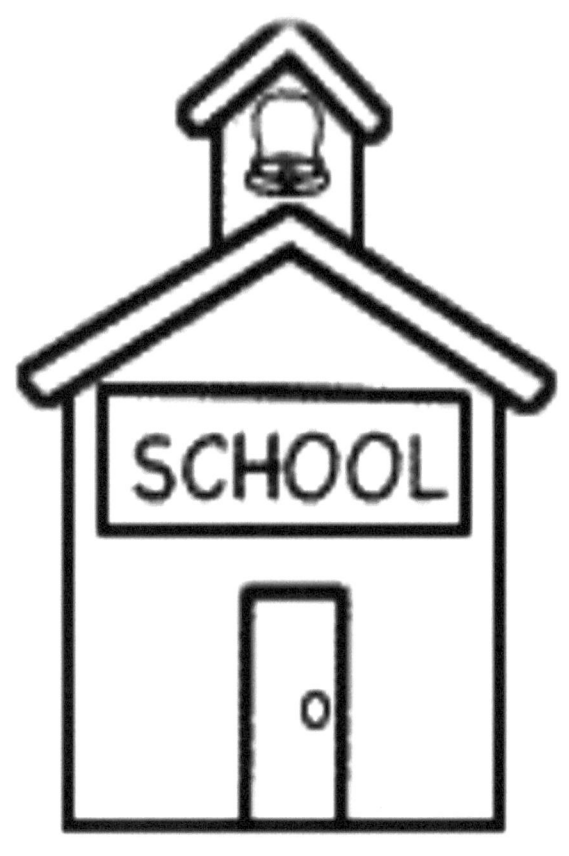

Finish

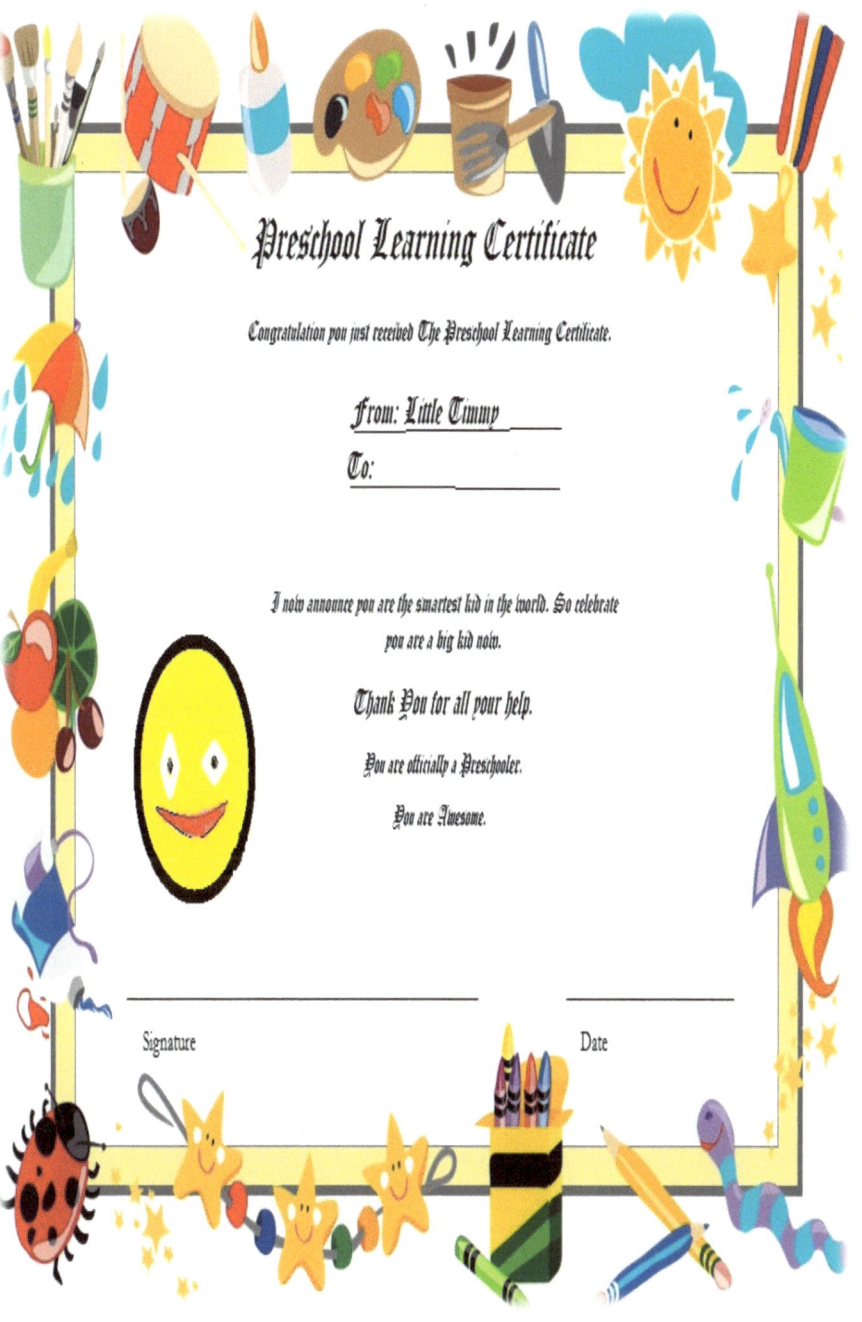

Preschool Learning Certificate

Congratulation you just received The Preschool Learning Certificate.

From: Little Timmy_____

To: _____

I now announce you are the smartest kid in the world. So celebrate you are a big kid now.

Thank You for all your help.

You are officially a Preschooler.

You are Awesome.

_____
Signature

_____
Date